Beekeeping for
Beginners

The Guide to Keeping Bees and Harvesting
Your Honey In Your Backyard

Sally R. Ball

Beekeeping For Beginners

Beekeeping For Beginners

Beekeeping For Beginners

Description

Beekeeping for Beginners is designed to introduce people of all backgrounds to beekeeping as a hobby. By the time you have completed this book, you will be able to set up a honey bee hive on your property, even in your backyard. You will understand the difference between honeybees and other types of bees. You will also gain effective knowledge of the honeybee life cycle and behavior.

All aspects necessary to set up a running honey bee hive will be covered in this book, from obtaining the hive box, to installing a queen and harvesting honey. Beekeeping is an exciting endeavor that anyone with the right knowledge can partake in. This book will provide you with all of the information you need to set up a honey bee hive and maintain it from one year to the next. The following subjects will be covered in this book:

- Introduction to honeybees, including the different honeybee species and how honeybees are different from other bees
- Honeybee social structure and lifecycle
- Honeybee communication
- The ins and outs of honeybee equipment
- The basic equipment you will need to set up your hive
- Attracting bees and obtaining a queen
- Harvesting honey and wax from your hive
- Inspecting your hive
- The costs of setting up and maintaining a hive
- Protecting yourself and other safety concerns

Beekeeping For Beginners

- Seasonal issues in beekeeping

These subjects and many more will be covered in *Beekeeping for Beginners*, leaving you confident enough to begin your forays into beekeeping as a productive and exciting hobby. It won't be long before you feel confident enough to help your neighbors set up hives of their own. It all starts with educating yourself on the subject and this book is the perfect place to start.

Bluesource And Friends

This book is brought to you by Bluesource And Friends, a happy book publishing company.

Our motto is **"Happiness Within Pages"**

We promise to deliver amazing value to readers with our books.

We also appreciate honest book reviews from our readers.

Connect with us on our Facebook page www.facebook.com/bluesourceandfriends and stay tuned to our latest book promotions and free giveaways.

Don't forget to claim your FREE books!

Brain Teasers:

https://tinyurl.com/karenbrainteasers

Harry Potter Trivia:

https://tinyurl.com/wizardworldtrivia

Sherlock Puzzle Book (Volume 2)

https://tinyurl.com/Sherlockpuzzlebook2

Also check out our best seller book

https://tinyurl.com/lateralthinkingpuzzles

Introduction

Congratulations on getting *Beekeeping for Beginners*. The chapters in this book will introduce you to beekeeping as a pastime, leaving you ready to set up a hive in your backyard if you so desire.

As a pastime, beekeeping has been known for thousands of years. The Ancient Egyptians and Greeks kept honeybees for their honey, and the idea of the industrious honeybee most likely dates back to ancient times. The great general Napoleon Bonaparte chose the bee as his symbol, as the image of fierceness and determination that was associated with the bee was one that he hoped to lend to his dynasty. Men and women around the world have long been fascinated with bees.

Perhaps one of the most interesting things about beekeeping is the bees themselves. Many go into beekeeping because they are drawn to the curious ability of honeybees to create honey. In fact, there are thousands of species of bees found all around the world, not all of which create honey. Honeybees are peculiar (and special) not only because they create honey from the pollen they collect from flowers, but also because of their complex and curious social structure.

Although some species of bee are solitary, the honeybee is known for its complex social structure with the queen at its apex. Indeed, this is one of the things most commonly known about honeybees and a fact which continues to fascinate. The complex structure of the honeybee hive runs like a well-oiled machine, allowing the bees to work as a group to collect nectar from flowers in the environment and to return to the hive where they turn that nectar into honey.

The bees do not merely make honey for our enjoyment. The honey serves an essential purpose: to allow the bees to survive through winter without access to food sources from the outside. This represented an evolutionary step forward for honeybees, as solitary bee species were unable to generate food sources large enough to allow a great number of bees in a social group to survive through winter. Although there are many types of bees outside the honeybee group which form hives, in many of these species only the queen survives through winter.

So, honeybees took a giant leap forward when they learned to make honey. As a beekeeper, you too can harness this bee ability to provide honey for your own table or for family and friends. As you may know, beekeeping is not only a pastime. Many people successfully make a living as beekeepers, keeping enough hives to be able to provide adequate amounts of honey for sale. Even in developing countries, the beekeeper is known, often traveling through town with his bucket of honey with the occasional honeycomb chunk inside.

Beekeeping For Beginners

In this book, *Beekeeping for Beginners*, you will learn how you too can benefit from the industry of honeybees. This may involve you learning a little industry yourself, as you gain knowledge of what honeybees are, how they work, how you can work with them, and how you can gain joy out of beekeeping. We will take you through the ins and outs of this pastime, from the basics of honeybees to beekeeping equipment, handling honeybees, and maintaining the hive over the winter. We will even review some of the frequently asked questions that men and women often have about beekeeping.

But first, it is important for the beginner to learn a little bit more about bees, honeybees in particular, as they will be your friends throughout this long journey. Many of you plan to set up a beehive in your backyard, so it would behoove you to learn a little more about your future neighbors. Therefore, we will begin our beekeeping journey with an introduction to honeybees.

Chapter 1

Introduction to Honeybees

Honeybee Basics

The first question to answer about honeybees is whether or not they should be referred to as honeybee or honey bee. This question really pivots on whether or not honeybees, as they are commonly known, are different from other bees in general, whether they are a special type of distinct bee, or merely just one among the thousands of species of bees. Indeed, of the approximately 20,000 known species of bee, the Western honey bee, or *Apis mellifera*, is just one, although it is perhaps the most commonly known. Debate aside, these bees are still commonly known as honeybee (one word) and will generally be referred to as such in this book.

Beekeeping For Beginners

As mentioned previously, beekeeping has been known from practically the beginnings of recorded history. They've been documented in cave paintings, Ancient Egyptian hieroglyphics, and various inscriptions from Egypt, Mesopotamia, and Greece. Indeed, some remains from the Middle East suggest that people in this region became so proficient that a single beekeeping operation might have been able to harvest honey from as many as 1 million bees.

Wherever honeybees were kept, they were valued, and ancient peoples kept records of how they harvested honey and wax from beehives. There are two main species of domesticated honeybee from which these substances are obtained presently. These species are *Apis mellifera* and *Apis cerana*. *Apis mellifera* is the so-called Western honey bee and is the main species of domesticated bee known in the West, although like its Asian counterpart, *Apis cerana*, there are notable subspecies.

Domestication of the Western honey bee must have occurred several thousands of years ago, as remains of honey from the tombs of Egyptian pharaohs suggest that the harvesting of honey was a very active endeavor that was already well-understood at this period. Indeed, this assessment is corroborated by records from Egypt and the Near East, which describe how beekeepers in this time managed to successfully harvest honey. Just as many beekeepers do today, smoking the hive was a common technique as it disorients the bees by making the pheromones produced by the queens useless.

Apis mellifera, the type of honeybee that you are most likely to domesticate in your beekeeping beginnings, is commonly reared in the United States and other countries of Western cultural origin. In East Asia, another species called *Apis cerana* is known. This species continues to be reared in spite of some of the advantages of *Apis mellifera*, because this latter species is vulnerable to attack and destruction by predators in the East Asian region, like wasps and hornets.

The situation of the honeybee and their classification becomes further muddled when one considers that there are other species of bees that produce honey, as well as species that are domesticated. In certain areas of Latin America, a genus of bees that produce honey called *Melipona* has been commercially sourced, although they are considered less commercially important than the two aforementioned species of honeybee. Later on, we will delve into the many other species of honeybee by way of comparison.

To summarize the honeybee picture, we can say that although there are several species of bee that produce honey, as well as bees that are domesticated. The domesticated honeybee that is used in beekeeping falls under the taxonomic genus *Apis* and consists of two major species:

- *Apis mellifera* (Western honey bee)
- *Apis cerana* (Eastern honey bee)

In this book, we will be dealing with the Western honey bee, *Apis mellifera*, as this is the commonly domesticated honeybee of the United States, other English-speaking countries, and most Western countries in general. There are other species of bee that produce honey or are domesticated for pollination purposes, but they are outside of the scope of this book. Before we delve into some of the specifics of the Western honey bee, it is important to note some basics of their social structure. The Western honeybee is divided into three general castes that we will learn more about later. These three castes are:

- Queen
- Worker
- Drone

The balance between these three castes is what allows bee colonies to grow large and produce honey that humans can use. The queen is the leader of the colony. She is also the largest member of the colony, making her easily distinguishable from the others. An existing queen produces a pheromone called queen substance that prevents the other females from full maturation while also controlling the drones. In reality, queen substance is most likely several pheromones that serve different purposes.

It is the female drones that perform the work of foraging for the bee colony. They do the heavy lifting both inside and outside of the colony. The drones are male, and they result from eggs that the queen lays that are unfertilized. It is believed that the only purpose of the drones in the bee colony is to procreate with the queen, which they undertake on a mating flight. A queen lays eggs and decides whether to fertilize them or not, based on the needs of the colony. This fertilization decision is very important as it affects the balance of male drones and female workers in the honeybee colony.

Honeybees have several means of communication or language. A Nobel Prize was awarded to Karl von Frisch for his studies of the dances that honeybees utilize to communicate with one another, namely the waggle dance and the round dance. Honeybees utilize these dances to communicate sources of food to one another. Honeybee queens notably make sounds called piping that has been actively studied. Mated queens make a tooting sound, particularly when a new queen has arrived in a hive or if there is more than one queen. Some scientists have postulated that this may represent a form of a battle cry.

Brief Discussion of the Origin of Honeybees

The Western honey bee is a little bit of an enigma as its genetic history is not entirely clear. It is believed that all members of the genus *Apis* originated in Southeast Asia, while the Western honey bee in particular (*Apis mellifera*) is believed to have surfaced in Eastern Africa, from where it eventually was cultivated in Northern Africa, Arabia, other areas of the Near East, and the Mediterranean region. There have been other honeybee species throughout the ages, and they are known to us from the fossil records. Currently, honeybees are divided into three clades for the purposes of classification:

- *Megapis* (giant honeybees)
- *Microapis* (dwarf honeybees)
- *Apis* (domesticated honeybees)

Beekeeping For Beginners

Within the genus *Apis* are the truly domesticated honeybees. Although the clade Apis also includes close relatives of the two primary domesticated honeybee species, *Apis mellifera* and the Western honey bee, it is interesting as the passage of time which led to this species originating in Africa (though its ancestors came from Asia) is not known.

What is known is that since its development as a species, *Apis mellifera* has had a close relationship with humans right up to the present. It represents the major species of domesticated honeybee. Apis mellifera is the species of honeybee that has been most consistently documented throughout the ages, going back to the Ancient Egyptians, and it is perhaps the only species that has been widely propagated outside its native area.

Types of Bees

There are about 20,000 known species of bees at present, and it is likely that more species will be described as scientists explore more deeply into remote areas in parts of the world, like Asia and Africa, which may not have been adequately studied. Honeybees and bumblebees are perhaps the best known, and they are closely related to other insects like ants and wasps. It is interesting to speculate on the evolutionary origin of bees, though it is outside the scope of this work. Some believe that bees are descended from wasps that preyed on other insects. At some point in history, these bee ancestors switched from consuming other insects to consuming pollen as a primary food source.

Although delving deeply into the different types of bees is not the intention of this work, it is useful to briefly explore this subject for the purposes of understanding the Western honey bee (the *honeybee* of this work). It may come as a surprise to some to learn that not all bees are social and not all bees consume honey. There are many solitary bee species. As one might imagine, a solitary bee is not likely to make honey, as this food source serves the primary purpose of feeding a colony through winter.

Some bees build their nests underground or directly into trees. Other species of bee are stingless. Some types of bee outside the more commonly known honeybees include the so-called mason bees, mining bees, plasterer bees, carpenter bees, and leafcutter bees. Some of these bees closely resemble our image of the Western honey bee while others bear little similarity, differing in size, color, and other variables.

Although honeybees have a fairly rigid and complex life cycle, it does bear some similarity to the general life cycle of bees as a group. Bees lay eggs, the eggs develop through pupal and larval stages, and then the eggs hatch and begin a process where the males seek females for mating. Immature bees often remain in this stage through winter, and the males may mature first, allowing them to be ready to seek out females for their mating flight.

Honeybee Hives and Queens

Now that we are familiar with bees as a particular (and curious) group of insects, we can learn specifically about the subject of this book: the honeybee. As you should have realized by this point, honeybees are unique among bee species because they do two things: they produce honey and they are domesticated. As we mentioned earlier, there are two main species of domesticated honeybee, but we will be dealing here with the Western honey bee, or *Apis mellifera*.

At the center of the honeybee hive is the queen. Like it or not, she is the most important member of the colony because she lays the eggs that allow the colony to continue, and she also produces pheromones that regulate the behavior of all the other members. Although this type of picture is true for other bees, because honeybee colonies can grow so large, the role of the queen becomes perhaps more important, especially when contrasted with bees that form groups of perhaps a few dozen members, or are solitary.

A honeybee colony can have tens of thousands of bees. The bees fall into the three groups mentioned previously: queen, workers, and drones. Although the queen is perhaps the single most significant individual in the colony, much of the work to sustain the colony is done by the workers. The worker bees are the ones that go out and produce pollen and then return to the bee to make honey, wax, and other important materials in the hive.

Still, first, let us deal with the queen. The queen has her own life cycle that is closely related to that of her hive. A new queen just emerged from her cell is a virgin queen. This distinction is important because other residents of the hive often will not recognize a virgin queen as a queen, even though she is larger than a worker, and this prevents her from being attacked. This is significant because if you are introducing a queen into an already established colony (after the loss of a queen), she should be a virgin in order to enhance the probability of survival.

After a queen emerges from her cell, she often seeks out other virgin queen rivals and destroys them. Eventually, she goes on her mating flight, in which she will mate with usually between ten and twenty drones. A virgin queen will initially not release much in the way of pheromones, which is part of the reason why she may not be recognized by workers, though she will release more pheromones over time. One important thing to note is that a virgin queen is a female that emerges from a queen cell after a previous queen die. This means that there may be several virgin queens in this period, but only one will become the new queen.

As mentioned in passing before, unfertilized eggs of the queen become male drones while fertilized eggs (fertilized from drone sperm) become workers and potential queens. If the virgin queen is prevented from going on a mating flight, she will only be able to lay drone eggs, which usually will cause the death of the hive as there will be no workers to complete the necessary hive functions.

As the queen gets older, she produces less in the way of pheromones. This prevents her from being able to control the other bees, which may lead to her being superseded. A queen is superseded when she is replaced by the bees in the colony. A queen bee can also be superseded by the beekeeper by damaging one of her legs, for example. A new queen will emerge from larval cells that have been fed ample amounts of royal jelly, a substance high in protein that is produced from workers' glands. If there are no queen larvae available when a queen dies, workers will feed worker cells large amounts of royal jelly to procure a new queen.

Even though the queen is larger than the other residents of the hive, it may be difficult to find her rapidly, so some beekeepers choose to mark her for the purposes of easy identification. The second most important caste in the hive is the worker. The workers perform a large variety of tasks aside from just collecting pollen. They also are engaged in various duties in the hive, including distributing hormones that the queen produces that prevent other workers from laying queen larvae (eggs that can develop into queens).

Two of the more important tasks of the workers are the storage and formation of beeswax. Beeswax is used to build the combs and cells of the hive, both necessary for meeting the requirements of the hive, including storage of eggs and honey. One last note about honeybee queens and workers is the act of swarming. Swarming is the act of forming a new colony, and this most commonly happens when an existing colony divide.

Beekeeping as a Pastime

In order to keep bees for leisure, it is crucial to understand their life cycle. We hope that, at this point, you have a sense of the main players of the hive and how they interact together. This is important for anyone who plans to keep bees to know, as their hive can quickly fail if a queen dies suddenly without new queen larvae available, or if a queen is unable to produce workers. A successful beekeeping venture must have all of these players—queen, workers, and drones—in place from the very beginning in order to survive.

A successful beekeeping endeavor must also have the necessary components of a hive to be viable. Honeybees need a place to store honey and eggs in order to function. If the honeybees are not able to do these things, the colony will fail. For this reason, commercially available hives must be able to replicate the basic functions of naturally-created hives. Typically, commercial hives attempt to do this while allowing the beekeeper to easily access the bees and their honey.

Chapter 2

The Basics of Beekeeping Equipment

It is easy to underestimate the importance of bees to agriculture. Some important agricultural products in the United States require bees for pollination. One of the more significant of these products is the almond, part of the lucrative almond industry in the state of California. Almonds are pollinated by bees, so almond farmers have to maintain a certain ratio of beehives to acres of farmland. For your purposes as a beginner, the main thing to note here is that beekeeping is not all that uncommon nor particularly expensive.

Although this will be delved into more in a bit, what the beehive needs to survive is a source of food (typically in the form of flowers the workers forage for pollen) and a hive that is protected from the elements and predators. This means, for you, that you either have to be near to an area where the bees can realistically forage for pollen or be willing to provide a food source for yourself. Therefore, setting up a beehive on the balcony of your New York City apartment is probably not the best idea. In this situation, you will not only be failing to provide your bees with access to foraging material, but you would also be creating a pest for your neighbors.

Obtaining a Hive

Humans have been obtaining bee products like honey and wax from constructed hives for thousands of years. The ancient peoples of Egypt and Mesopotamia are known to have constructed hives for the purposes of rearing large numbers of bees in a single location. This pursuit is still active today, as beekeepers keep large numbers of beehives for the purposes of agricultural production, such as in the case of blueberries, almonds, cloves, and the like. For the man or woman choosing beekeeping for leisure, these large set-ups are probably not in your future, but you should have a basic understanding of constructed hives.

There are many different types of commercially available hives, many of them made out of wood. Most of the beehives that are set up or transported to commercial agricultural ventures are the simple and basic wooden variety. These are perfectly viable hives that accomplish the tasks that a beekeeper requires of a hive: being able to provide water and food if necessary, to the hive, and protecting the hive from predators and the elements.

With that said, there is a growing industry of commercially-produced hives for sale, that is, hives that have been specially designed for the purposes of making the beekeeper's job easier. Many of these hives are made out of artificial materials and they come in a variety of price ranges. What is important for you to know are the basic components of a beehive (also called a bee box or a hive kit), so that you can obtain one that allows you to set up your hive right where you need it to be.

Some bee boxes will require some assembling, while others will be shipped already assembled. Price ranges may vary but be prepared to spend in the range of two hundred dollars and up, not to mention any investment in time that may be necessary. A more complex and expensive bee box may require more time to assemble, though some of these may come with the assembly already completed.

Some people choose to construct their own bee box or beehive, and this is a good opportunity to delve more deeply into some of the components of a good constructed beehive or bee box. Although, at first glance, it may seem that a good bee box would be just that, a box for the bees to build their hive into, a bee box has several important components that encourage the bees to produce honey and wax and allow you to obtain them.

The important components of a bee box or constructed hive are listed below:

- Hive stand
- Bottom board
- Entrance reducer
- Deep super
- Deep super frames
- Queen excluder
- Honey super

- Honey super frames
- Inner cover
- Outer cover

Hives should be lifted up off of the ground and that is what the hive stand is for. The rest of your hive kit will rest on this stand. The bottom board is the bottom-most part of your bee box other than the hive stand. The bottom board is a piece of wood that serves as a route of entry for the bees. It has an entrance reducer that prevents insects and other predators that prey on bees from entering the hive set.

The deep super is one of the two main boxes that comprise your bee box. This box has frames, known commonly as deep super frames, that are slotted into a rack in the box, onto which the bees build their wax for the colony. Eight to ten frames are normal for a deep super box. Between the deep super and the honey super is the queen excluder. This is basically a screen with holes large enough for workers, but too small for a queen. The queen excluder is put in place to prevent queens from planting their brood in the honey box.

The honey super has frames just like the deep super, and it is in these frames that the bees will deposit their honey. The frames can be taken out to harvest the honey later on. The honey super should not be too large as it will become filled with honey, and you need to be able to lift it realistically. On top of the honey super are usually two lids or covers that are designed to protect the honey portion of the box, as well as to keep the elements out of the bee box altogether.

These are the basic components of most bee boxes. Commercially-available bee boxes may differ slightly in terms of the materials that the components are constructed of, and how complex certain features like the entrance reducer are. Many bee boxes also allow you to increase the number of frames or add more super boxes, as the need requires. The bee box has basic components (already mentioned), which means that the industrious carpenter or craftsman can build his or her own from wood if they would like.

The Internet is a good resource to get an idea of the overall dimensions of these components as well as an idea of what they should look like. Remember, the idea is not only to be able to obtain honey from your introduced bee colony, but also to meet the basic needs of the bees so that they are able to carry on life as they would in a normal colony.

Harvesting Honey from a Hive

As you can probably imagine from the description of the beehive or bee box components that we mentioned above, it is not difficult to harvest honey from the hive if you are using that basic setup. The setup is designed to allow you to easily access the honey box and remove the frames containing the honey as needed.

There are several important things you need to know prior to extracting honey from the hive, including when the time to extract honey will be. You want to extract honey after the bees have had time to build honeycombs, but before they have stopped foraging and depositing honey. This is to ensure that there are ample supplies of honey in your box before you harvest it. It is a good idea to harvest honey in midsummer, or at least before the fall so that you have ample stores to access.

Bees generally forage in the daylight hours of about eight or nine in the morning, until about four or five in the afternoon. In terms of time of day, this is a good time of day to harvest your honey. There may still be some bees around, so ancient methods of removing bees still come in handy. This includes smoking the hive to stun the bees, by blocking the queen's pheromones. You can also use a blower to blow any remaining bees away from the box before you access the honey.

This is a good time to talk about protective gear. It is important that your skin is not exposed (for the most part) when accessing the hive. This is especially true of the face and neck regions. You can wear a beekeeping suit or outfit with a mask to prevent bees from accessing these areas. You also should consider wearing gloves, although some advanced beekeepers choose to go without them. As a beginner, it is probably a good idea not to forego the gloves. To prevent skin from being exposed, it is a good idea to wear long pants (or overalls) and boots in addition to the protective gear.

Now that you have protective gear on, you are ready to harvest the honey. Access the honey super by removing the inner and outer covers. We talked about smoking, and it is a good idea to smoke and wait a minute before you access each of the covers. Remove each frame individually. It is a good idea to transport the frames away from the hives so as not to attract the bees back as you are removing and extracting the honey.

We will talk more about harvesting honey later, but you may want to transport the frames in a cart to a shed or barn. You will use a knife to first uncap the wax and then remove the honeycombs from the frame. The honeycombs will be emptied into a bucket or other receptacle. Repeat the process for each frame, making sure to replace the frames with new ones, rather than putting the ones you have removed honey from back.

There are different ways of extracting the honey from the harvested honeycombs. You can use a device called an extractor or you can extract the honey manually. Extracted honey should be stored in jars. A common way to do this is to strain the honey through cheesecloth as you place it in jars. It is a good idea to leave some honey remaining in the hives for the bees. Having all of their honey removed may enrage them.

Chapter 3

Setting Up Your Hive and the Economic Aspects of Beekeeping

The first step to setting up a hive, after you have installed the hive box, is obtaining bees. Many people choose to purchase bees while those in rural areas often attract bees. We touched on the subject of swarms briefly. Swarms form generally when a colony splits or if a colony moves to a new location. Worker bees called scouts will look for a new location for a hive before the swarm actually moves to that location. Many beekeepers have their own special way of attracting a swarm to their hive and there is no general consensus on how to do it.

Commercially-available products marketed as hive baits can be purchased. Some beekeepers create their own concoctions designed to attract bees to the hive. This often includes particularly fragrant substances like lemongrass, which are designed to draw scout bees as well as swarms. Some beekeepers attract swarms merely by choosing a good location or setting up their hive at an ideal height. Although the general recommendation is that hives should be elevated from the ground, there is no consensus about how high they should be lifted, with some recommending as high as several feet.

Overview of the Economic Aspects of Beekeeping

Most people reading this are choosing to go into beekeeping as a pastime, not as a commercial pursuit, so it stands to reason that you are seeking to embark on this process as cost-effectively as possible. This means striking a good balance between investment into this endeavor and the potential payout. You will have to invest some funds into purchasing or building a hive, though these expenses should not be exorbitant. You can purchase a single constructed hive for a couple of hundred dollars or build your own out of simple products.

If you are choosing to purchase bees, the basic investment will be about three hundred or four hundred dollars, not counting the cost of protective gear, equipment, and the like. Some of these costs can be defrayed if you are able to construct the hive yourself.

Beekeeping For Beginners

Most likely you will be harvesting the honey for yourself, though many who go into beekeeping for leisure choose to sell their honey. You might be able to balance out some of the costs of your beekeeping by selling your honey, though the costs of beekeeping are really minimal if you do it the right way. Some of the things that you will have to invest in are:

- Bee box
- Protective gear
- Storage receptacles
- Smoker
- Bee food
- Queen

Attracting a Swarm

We have briefly mentioned some of the steps involved in swarming and attracting a swarm, although doing this successfully requires more knowledge. We understand why bees swarm, but when do they swarm? This generally varies by geographic location as swarming can be dependent on the weather. Bees will swarm earlier in warmer regions and later in more temperate ones. Honeybees will swarm as early as February in the deep south and as late as May in the mid-Atlantic. You want to have your hive box setup before the normal swarming period in your part of the country. A good guide for most parts of the United States is March or April, but some research here can go a long way.

An important aspect of setting up the bee box is choosing a good location. Bees like sunlight so setting up the bee box facing East or South can be a good idea. With that said, the spot should not be directly in the light, and a little shade is important. The bee box should be elevated off of the ground at least a foot. If you already have a swarm in the area, many beekeepers recommend setting up the bee near to this pre-existing swarm. Finally, an area that is exposed to the elements, such as an open area far from trees or cover, is generally not a good idea.

A nifty trick that some beekeepers in the business use is to keep an old frame from an older bee box. Bees like the familiar, so a frame from a hive that other bees have successfully deposited wax and honey in is likely to be more attractive to bees than a bee box made up of entirely new products. That is not to say that if you choose to build a bee box you will not attract bees but adding something old to your new setup can go a long way.

Installing the Queen

There is much more to the subject of installing a queen than meets the eye. Many swarming bees will already have a queen, while a colony already in place may have larvae in the hive with the potential of developing into queens. Most commercial beekeepers and many beekeepers going into the field as a pastime choose to purchase a queen. This involves receiving a queen in a queen cage, a queen that is already in a position to be installed in a colony.

There is some debate about whether a new queen should be an already mated queen or a virgin. Although a mated queen from a different colony has the potential of being attacked by workers, some beekeepers have found a high rate of acceptance of mated queens. A virgin queen has not yet mated with drones and is unlikely to be attacked by workers.

As a beginner beekeeper, you have several options in terms of the queen. Assuming that your swarm does not already have a queen, you can capture a queen from another colony or purchase one. Some beekeepers that already have established colonies find it necessary to resort to these methods to replace a queen when they feel she is responsible for a failing colony, or if the colony has been struck by disease. This is called requeening and the process is similar to establishing a queen in a new colony, which will be discussed shortly.

A queen may develop naturally from the queen larvae that have been laid. The risks of allowing an already established colony to come up with its own queen are primarily that if the queen does not develop in time, she may not be able to fertilize eggs that she has lain, and the colony will die for lack of workers. Purchasing or capturing a queen circumvents this issue as such a queen should be able to get to work right away mating and laying eggs.

Additional queens are generally available for purchase, because a new swarm usually has several virgin queens available before one establishes dominance over the colony. However, most queens that are delivered are already mated and are shipped with a food source called queen candy, and with several worker attendants.

A queen will generally go on her mating flight three days after taking her place in the swarm. This timing is important as any delay may lead to an eventual absence of worker bees and the death of the colony. A mated queen may potentially lay eggs sooner, which will be good for your new colony. Once a purchased queen has arrived, you place her into the bee box. The queen is placed in her cage in between frames of a super. She is usually placed with her candy so that she has food while the bees take time to accept her.

Feeding Your Bees

The last subject to discuss here is feeding your bees. Honey is produced by bees as a food source, but a swarm that has just settled in a hive naturally would not have any honey in place. For this reason, purchasing food will be important for new beekeepers. There are many commercially available foods sources for bees. Some can be inserted into your bee box in the form of a frame (although, there are other means as well). You can also purchase fondant cheaply, which we will discuss later when we talk about seasonal issues. You will have to make sure that your bee box has the dimensions to be able to accept the food.

Once the colony is active and has begun making honey, you will no longer need to provide them with food. Again, when you get to the point of removing honey from the hive that the bees have produced, it is a good idea to leave some behind. Once you have an active colony and are in the process of potentially setting up more colonies, this process may become easier as you may already have frames filled with honey available to install in a new hive.

Chapter 4

Safety Concerns in Beekeeping

Basic Safety Measures

The issue of safety in beekeeping is an interesting one. Some beekeepers believe it is important to be stung once in a while, as this builds up your body's natural resistance to the venom in the sting. Because the bee venom contains pathogens, your body builds up antibodies in the form of IgG, and therefore, eventually builds up resistance to the effect of the sting. This is why you may see beekeepers accessing their beehives with protective gear covering their bodies, but without gloves.

As a beginning beekeeper, it will be important for you to wear the full get-up of protective gear for your safety. This book assumes that you are a complete beginner who is unfamiliar with most of the finer details of beekeeping and have not built up any sort of natural immunity to bees. Although beekeeping is an activity that has been undertaken for thousands of years and can be handled perfectly safely, there are some concerns that you need to take into consideration.

The first concern is that bees do sting, and you need to protect yourself. Besides the obvious protection of wearing protective gear, there are other precautions that you should take, some of which have been mentioned previously. These precautions include accessing the hives at times when most of the worker bees will be outside of the hive foraging, typically between nine in the morning and five in the afternoon. You also want to use a bee smoker to remove any bees that are still in the hive. Also, you can use an air blower to physically blow bees away from the hive as you are accessing it.

The other aspect of safety to note, is what to do if you are stung by a bee. Bee stings can be painful, especially if you have not been stung before. A sting will leave a stinger in the affected area, so you want to remove the sting without stimulating the bee to inject any more venom into the site. Scraping or swiping rather than grabbing is usually an effective way to do this. Like other injuries that involve some form of skin penetration or physical trauma, washing the area with water and soap helps to cleanse the area and reduce the risk of irritation.

To reduce swelling, taking a cold cloth or some ice and applying it to the area usually does the trick. As mentioned, you should find stings affect you less and less if you do happen to be stung more than once.

Common Issues in Beekeeping

Honeybees are preyed on by other larger insects. We mentioned briefly that bees may have evolved from wasps that preyed on other insects. Over time, bees lost the desire (or ability) to prey on other insects, but wasps are still around as a potential predator. Both wasps and hornets prey on honeybees, which is part of the reason why *Apis mellifera*, the Western honey bee, has not become popular in some parts of the world, like Japan. There are other predators of bees like certain species of moth and the terrifyingly named European beewolf.

The European beewolf is a species of wasp. The females of this wasp species hunt honeybees, eventually paralyzing them and taking them back to their nest to serve as supper for their larvae. Although this is a startling example of a honeybee predator, it is one that you as a beekeeper can do little about. Predators that hunt bees while foraging cannot be circumvented, although you can make attempts to prevent predators from entering the hive.

Positioning the hive at a certain height above the ground while also using the recommended setup of hive components that we mentioned previously will serve as an important mechanism of preventing critters from entering your hive. Other than insects, birds and frogs also prey on bees, and besides setting up your hive in the best way possible, there is little that you can do to stop them.

Besides predators, other issues impacting bee survival are other species of bee, such as the so-called Africanized honeybees, and environmental factors like pesticides. Indeed, one of the advantages of beekeeping in a backyard rather than a large-scale farming area is that your hive will be further removed from insecticides, pesticides, and other harmful substances that are rampant in many agricultural areas in the United States. Feral bees that can hybridize with *Apis mellifera* are a concern as they can displace native species and are slightly more aggressive to humans.

A very important step that you can take in protecting your hive and the bees inside is to perform regular inspections. What you are looking for in your inspections is that the hive is free of invasive pests, the structure is intact and functioning as it should, and that all the members are present and doing their jobs. To reiterate, it is essential that a bee colony have a functioning queen, and colonies without them can die out in a short period, as they may be unable to produce workers.

Environmental Concerns

As many of you interested in beekeeping may also have an interest in environmental matters, it is important to briefly touch on the subject of some of the environmental concerns. Pesticides and insecticides can have positive and negative effects on honeybees. Honeybees can be damaged by exposure to insecticides, but they can also benefit from insecticides that target predators of bees, such as certain spiders and mites.

Beekeeping For Beginners

An impact of insecticides that may come as a surprise is that, as insects build resistance to insecticides, honeybee numbers have tended to drop in some areas, as these pests have begun a resurgence and have resumed targeting their former prey. Many people desire to go into beekeeping as naturally and holistically as possible. Although there is no consensus on what natural beekeeping it is, certain practices like artificial insemination of hives, moving hives frequently, and feeding hives with artificial substances tend to be avoided by natural practitioners.

Chapter 5

Seasonal Issues in Beekeeping and Harvesting Honey

It is important to inspect a new hive. After you have installed your queen, you want to make sure that the colony has accepted her, and there will be signs of this in the hive. Some new beekeepers will look for the queen during their inspection to determine that the hive has accepted the new queen, but if you find the presence of eggs in your hive, this is a good sign that the hive has taken to her.

For a new beekeeper, it may be difficult to distinguish the queen from the drones. Drones may seem to be large like a queen, but a queen actually has a longer body than both drones and workers. Her body is slender and long, where the body of the drone is plumper. Drones also can be distinguished from the queen by their large eyes, giving them a very distinct appearance. Even though the queen has a distinct appearance, some seasoned beekeepers may choose to mark the queen to make rapid identification of her easier.

A Quick Word About Drones

As mentioned in the introduction, the primary role of drones in the colony is to mate with the queen. The queen also has the ability to determine if the eggs she lays will be workers or drones, by her choice of whether to fertilize them or not. The presence of drones in a new hive is a sign that a hive is healthy and thriving, as the queen has invested in the creation of drones. This is a sign that the colony is able to accommodate members that do not forage and essentially draw resources away from the hive.

Removing Frames from The Hive

Honey and wax are harvested by removing the frames from the two supers that you have in your bee box. Accessing the hive is best accomplished by a process that involves smoking the hive at every stage to minimize your contact with bees and reduce the likelihood of a sting. Once you have removed both the outer and inner cover of the hive (which is usually accomplished using a tool to remove the tight inner cover), you can begin removing the frames.

The frames should be removed one by one, as frames filled with honey are likely to be heavy. How you harvest the frames is up to you but taking them to an area like a barn or a shed that is some distance away from the bee box is a good idea. It may be a good idea to have a cart to place the frames in, and then push the cart to the area where you will be extracting the honey.

The honey is removed by using a knife, fork, or other objects to force the honey off of the frame. The honey will be in honeycombs that will be crushed in the process of extracting the honey. It is a good idea to remove the honey from the frames into a bucket or other receptacle that can then be fed into an extractor. An extractor is not absolutely necessary. As mentioned, some people choose to do the extraction process manually.

Most people who have more than one hive choose to invest in an extractor. This is an easy way to obtain large amounts of honey quickly and simply from your several hives. As you will likely have a single hive and may be limited in space, you can spend some time learning how to extract honey without an extractor. There are some tips that may be helpful to you, such as using a hot knife to uncap the frames.

The uncapping from the frames will also reveal wax. People tend to focus on the honey, but the wax has many uses. Indeed, wax from honeybees has been used for thousands of years for a variety of purposes. Many conventional beekeepers keep the wax for use as furniture polish, sealant, and the like. Doing a little research can help you come up with ways of using this resource rather than wasting it.

Wintering Your Bees

One of your goals is to keep the bees alive through winter. Honeybees are able to do this naturally, but we are dealing with a constructed hive here so there are some things to keep in mind. The idea is essentially to keep the hive warm, to put some thought into the size of the hive (which shouldn't be as big of an issue for a new hive), and to put some thought into feeding the hive.

Of course, these are non-issues if you live in areas that do not get very cold, such as southern states that do not normally receive snow in the winter, or where temperatures do not typically drop below 60 degrees. For states that expect snow, such as far northern states, mid-Atlantic states, the Midwest, and the like, you may want to take the following steps:

- Relocate hive(s) to a warmer area to receive full sun.
- Block the hives from the wind.
- Switch from a larger entrance reducer to a smaller one.
- Purchase a hive cover to cover your hive.
- Provide food (many choose to purchase fondant inexpensively).
- Do not inspect the hive in the winter, but make sure bees are warm and fed.

Frequently Asked Questions

1. **Are there different types of bees?**

   There are thousands of different species of
   bees of which honeybees are only one.
   Western honey bees, or *Apis mellifera*, are
   perhaps the best-known bees because humans
   have used them as a source of honey for
   thousands of years. In ancient civilizations,
   people observed the ability of these bees to
   harvest pollen from their environment in
   order to make honey. This fascinated them
   not only from the standpoint of the honey,
   which they enjoyed, but also because of the
   intricate social pattern that is a hallmark of the
   species.

   But, in fact, honeybees are not the only
   species of bee. Many bees form colonies, but
   in some species, most of the drones do not
   survive the winter, as they lack a food source.

Many bee species are solitary. There may be different species of bee living in the same area unnoticed by the people around, who cannot tell the difference. Some bees even live underground.

2. **Why should I go into beekeeping?**

People go into beekeeping for different reasons. Some people choose to go into beekeeping for profit, as honey has been a staple source of sweetener for thousands of years. If you are reading this, you most likely plan to go into beekeeping as a hobby. Perhaps you would like to harvest your own natural honey without all the additives that are frequently found in most commercially-available honey. Perhaps you are interested in bees as a species, and you would like to learn more about them by having your own hive in your backyard.

There is no wrong reason to go into beekeeping. Indeed, the people who derive the most joy from beekeeping often have several reasons; not least of which is interest in bees. Let's face it, bees are interesting, and people have been fascinated by their industry throughout recorded history. It is important to remember that successful beekeeping will require some education on your part, which is what this book is for. You want to become familiar, not only with honeybees themselves, but their lifecycle and the ins-and-outs of the hive.

3. **Can I make money keeping bees?**

Beekeeping can be a profitable business. There are beekeepers around the world who are able to make and maintain a livelihood solely by keeping bees. Of course, it may take time for the beginner beekeeper to get to that stage, but it is not impossible, as many before you have done it. Most of you reading this are probably interested in beekeeping solely as a fun pastime, but if you decide to go into commercial beekeeping, this book can help prepare you for that.

One of the things to remember about commercial beekeeping, is that certain hive setups make the endeavor faster and more lucrative. A successful beekeeping operation will have hives that easily provide food for the bees and easily allow honey to be removed. Successful hives also are able to withstand the weather well enough that bees do not have to be replaced after the winter. It is also important to keep in mind how many bees you want in your hive.

4. **Is it expensive keeping honeybees?**
    There is some economic investment that goes into beekeeping, although it does not compare

with other agricultural pursuits like cattle ranching, for example. If you are beginning this book at this section, you will discover later that there is some equipment necessary for a successful beekeeping endeavor. Commercial beekeeping generally involves utilizing constructed hives.

There are many different hive kits to choose from, with some more expensive than others. These hive kits allow the beekeeper to easily have access to the bees, provide them with food, and easily harvesting the honey. Many hive kits are expandable, allowing you to keep more bees as you become more proficient and confident in beekeeping. Hive kits also are designed to withstand the weather, so that you can maintain your honeybee colony from one season to the next, benefitting both the bees and you.

5. Is beekeeping safe?

Beekeeping is safe enough that people have been able to do it successfully for thousands of years. Think about that for a minute: people were keeping bees even when they did not have all the fancy protective equipment that we have today. Some of this has to do with proper knowledge of how to interact with and handle bees. In reality, bees do not want to sting you. Stinging is a defensive mechanism that bees use when they feel their hive or queen is threatened.

If beekeeping was not safe, we would not be able to explain to you how to set up a beehive in your backyard, or other areas near where you and your family live. Like most living things on this planet, honeybees are able to live in equilibrium with their environment, meaning that they are only a nuisance when they have to be. The fact that people are able to take honey from hives at all and live to tell, suggests that honeybees can't be all that bad, can they?

6. **Is there anything I should know about inspecting my hive?**

Inspecting your hive is similar to accessing your hive as you would when removing frames of honey from the honey super. You want to choose a time in the day when the bees are out foraging. You also want to equip yourself with a smoker to remove any remaining bees from the hive. You basically want to smoke the hive before you remove the top cover. You will do it again after you remove the top cover, and then a third time after you remove the inner cover.

Take your time. After each smoking stage, you want to wait at least a minute for the bees to leave. During your inspection, you want to examine the frames. Perhaps during your inspection, you see that the queen that you purchased (and introduced) is out of her cage. This means that the cage can be discarded. Make sure that you reassemble the hive box correctly.

7. **I want to buy a manufactured hive kit. What kind of hive should I buy?**

    We have touched on the subject of commercially-available hives a few times in this book. There is an active market for commercial hives as many people decide to go into the pastime, and as the industry makes some advances and improvements on pre-existing models. Commercial hives differ in size, the material of construction, and, of course, cost. Some hives are made of wood, while some are made of synthetic plastics.

The choice of which hive is the best fit for you and your family, depends on a few different factors. How many bees do you plan to keep? Do you want a hive made out of wood or one made out of plastic? Do you want to be able to increase the number of bees you have over time without having to purchase an additional hive? How much money do you plan to spend on a hive? All of these are important questions to ask when considering which hive is a good fit for you.

8. Where should I set up my beehive?

This book assumes that you will be setting up your beehive in your backyard or another spot near your house, but there are many options in terms of places to set up your hive. Bees carefully choose their location for their hive, because they have certain needs in terms of access, size, proximity to other areas, temperature, dampness, and the like. As we have mentioned previously, there are many different types of bees. Some species of bee even live underground.

You may want to set up your beehive in your backyard, though there are other options as well, depending on the size of your property. As you can imagine, certain factors like temperature and protection from the elements are important. This is not only to encourage your bees to make honey, but for the basic need to keep the bees alive.

9. **Is it safe to have hives so near the house?**
Bees are generally not a danger to human beings unless an allergy exists. Of course, bees do sting, but honeybees are generally considered docile and typically will not sting humans unless threatened. In short, bees are safe to keep in your backyard as long as no one is allergic to their sting, and anyone

handling bees is properly educated and trained on how to deal with them. In reality, if you have a backyard with flowers, you may already have a hive nearby.

Indeed, some people occasionally stumble on a bee in their backyard without knowledge that they have a hive nearby. Even more than that, some people may be surprised that they have more than one species of bee in the area. What this means is that bees, honeybees in this case, are perfectly capable of living in equilibrium with humans. What's important for you as a beginner beekeeper to know, is how to interact with them effectively for your mutual benefit.

10. Why is it necessary to have a deep super and honey super instead of a single box?

The purpose of having two super boxes is so that there is an area for the queen to lay her eggs that is separate from where the workers are making and depositing honey. Otherwise, there will be eggs deposited together with honey, which will make the process of removing the honey from the bee box a cumbersome task. The boxes are designed to allow free movement of all except the queen throughout the hive. The queen is blocked by the queen excluder, which is placed between the deep super and the honey super.

11. **Am I harming the bees by keeping them?**
    In this day and age, many of us are concerned about reducing environmental impact and learning to live in a healthy balance with our environments. The question of whether it is beneficial to the bees themselves to be kept in a hive, as a pastime or commercially, is an

interesting one. The reality is that a beekeeper that has been educated well on the subject should be able to maintain a hive without unnecessary loss of life to the hive members.

Beekeeping as a pastime should not be harmful or detrimental to the bees if you are doing it properly. We hope that we have educated you enough on the subject to allow you to do that.

12. **How can I learn more about beekeeping?**
It may be a good idea to connect with a local beekeeper in your area or to join a beekeeping club.

13. **Why are honeybees so fascinating?**
This is not an easy question to answer. Many people are fascinated by honeybees because they have preconceived notions about non-

human life. Human beings are the smart ones, right? We build things, we have complex social relationships, and we grow crops for our own survival. It is more than a little fascinating to discover that there are other creatures on this earth with social structures as complex as our own, in a manner of speaking. In reality, the honeybee social structure is both complex and straightforward at once.

Nevertheless, that is not the only reason people find honeybees fascinating. Some people are entranced by the ability of bees to industriously forage for pollen and make honey. In doing this, bees not only create something that is delicious and nutritious to humans, but they also play an essential role in their environment, serving as vectors of pollination. Indeed, many flowering plants require bees for their own survival. Also, as human beings face questions of how we, too, can live in equilibrium with our environment, the example of the honeybee helps guide us in the right direction.

Conclusion

Thank you for completing *Beekeeping for Beginners*. We hope this book provided the information you need to feel confident enough to begin your forays into beekeeping.

Every person has their own reason to be interested in going into beekeeping. Some of you have been interested in the subject from childhood, nurturing a lifelong fascination for these small creatures that are able to so brilliantly create a substance as delicious as honey. Indeed, the work of honeybees even fascinated the ancients, with their notions about the industry of honeybees being passed on to us today. By keeping bees in your backyard, you are able to have some of that industry rub off on you while providing a natural source of honey for your table.

As we have seen in this book, honeybees are not the only bees, although they bear some similarities to their kindred. Out of the thousands of species of bees residing all over the world, honeybees are the most famous. Although, whether they are the most interesting is an interesting question for debate. Some bee species are solitary, some build their hives underground. Some bees bear little resemblance to the image of the bee that we have in our minds, based on that of the honeybee.

In this book, we introduced you to the life and times of the honeybee to help you understand the species better. This will allow you to interact effectively with these small creatures, which will benefit you and them for many years to come if you decide to continue forward in this pursuit. At the apex of the honeybee society is the queen who controls her members through an intricate system of pheromones and genetic differences. Queens emit a substance that prevents other females from full maturation, allowing there to be only one queen at a time in a honeybee colony.

It is important to understand honeybee society in order to be a beekeeper. It is also important to understand the equipment you will need to set up a shop, as well as how to keep yourself safe. Beekeeping is a perfectly safe pastime if you do it properly, and we hope that we have prepared you well to start your initial pursuit. As we have seen in this book, the best bet is probably to purchase a commercially-available hive, as these are designed to yield large amounts of honey. However, if you are more interested in beekeeping for knowledge or for fun, you have other options.

It is important that you and your honeybees are able to live in harmony together. The last thing you want is to invest all this time and energy in beekeeping only to have your bees perish. Beekeeping as a pastime should be a pleasurable pursuit, as you learn more about the bees. Although there may be some stumbles in your initial pursuits in beekeeping, as you become more knowledgeable and comfortable, you will find that beekeeping is not hard. Indeed, it can be a very rewarding endeavor.

We hope that you have enjoyed *Beekeeping for Beginners*. You should feel comfortable to begin your journey into this pastime, equipped with the knowledge of what honeybees are and how you can make them work for you (or with you), for the benefit of you both. At the end of the day, honeybees can be your domesticated commodity, but they can also be your friend.

Finally, if you enjoyed this book a review on Amazon would be appreciated!

Sally R. Ball

Connect with us on our Facebook page www.facebook.com/bluesourceandfriends and stay tuned to our latest book promotions and free giveaways.

www.ingramcontent.com/pod-product-compliance
Lightning Source LLC
Chambersburg PA
CBHW051357280526
45784CB00007B/2991